I0439650

Contents

Illustrations

Tables

Chapter 1

Introduction

Everybody thinks it's about guns and bombs. It isn't. It's about fuel and information. If you have enough fuel to keep moving, and you know what the other guy's doing, chances are you will win.

—Admiral Robbie Jackson, USN
Fictional character in Tom Clancy's book
Executive Orders

The epigraph above quite nicely gets across the essence of the Chairman's, Joint Chiefs of Staff (JCS), vision contained in *Joint Vision 2020*. In that document the US military has defined an operational goal for *full spectrum dominance*, to be achieved through dominant maneuver, precision engagement, focused logistics and full dimensional protection. Underlying each of the above concepts is the requirement for *decision superiority* over our adversaries through *information superiority*.[1] Full spectrum dominance is "the ability of US forces . . . to defeat any adversary and control any situation across the full range of military operations."[2] Decision superiority is defined as "better decisions arrived at and implemented faster than an opponent can react."[3] And information superiority, is "the capability to collect, process, and disseminate and uninterrupted flow of information while exploiting or denying an adversary's ability to do the same."[4] The first two terms are important because they describe the desired conditions and end results of actions taken by the US military. The third term,

1

information superiority, is considered key because this is where space-based intelligence, surveillance and reconnaissance (ISR) agencies—namely the National Imagery and Mapping Agency (NIMA), the National Reconnaissance Office (NRO), and the National Security Agency (NSA)—and their assets are able to contribute toward the JCS defined goal.

The Criticality of Space-based ISR

In the words of a recent congressional commission, "Space has proven to be the most effective means for gaining frequent, assured access to denied areas on a global basis."[5] These thoughts are certainly echoed by the landmark *Air Force 2025* study, "From space, one can observe what is occurring in all time zones. Its importance will only grow in the future. By 2025 it is very likely that space will be to the air as air is to cavalry today."[6] Senior leaders and noted authors have hailed space-based ISR capabilities as central to achieving a "new American way of war" that can "replace the need for overwhelming force with decisive knowledge-based action."[7]

This paper could be misconstrued as proposing that the only way to gather information is from space; however, that would be an error. There are many mechanisms by which to gather data and each medium (e.g., land, sea, air, space and "human") can and will be used by our nation to collect information. However, due to the unfettered view from space, its ability to look deep within a sovereign area without violating sovereignty, and the volume of data space assets are capable of collecting—space-based ISR is this paper's focus.

While certainly each service plays a role relative to space-ISR, the three major agencies are NIMA, NSA and NRO. NRO's focus is on the development and operations of the space-based ISR collection system. NIMA and NSA are focused on the tasking of the space-based ISR resources, and the processing, analysis and dissemination of the imagery and SIGINT data generated respectively.   Access to space and the cost to provide the ISR data is not cheap. Actual budget numbers for NIMA, NRO and NSA are classified, but open sources estimate that these three agencies account for approximately 45% of the annual $27 billion US IC budget.[8]   Because of the literal and unprecedented perspective provided by space-based ISR systems, their tremendous abilities and their value, NIMA, NRO, and NSA are directly tied to achieving the Chairman's vision.

Current Situation

In 1960 the worlds first imaging spy satellite, known as CORONA was launched. It was a film return system that brought exposed film negatives down from orbit in reentry capsules. These capsules had to be caught in mid-air over the Pacific Ocean by aircraft, and taken to a ground facility so the film they contained could be processed into pictures. This process would typically take days from the time of the first picture being taken to the time that any film was developed and delivered to an imagery analyst for exploitation.[9]

Today, without getting into the specific details that would make this paper classified, it is safe to say that our country has space-based ISR capabilities that are orders of magnitude better than those that existed in the early 1960s due to the ability to do near real-time imaging and space-based collection of signals intelligence (SIGINT).[10] Despite having these tremendous space-based ISR capabilities, there are quotes in the open press from Congressional members and senior military leaders describing serious problems with our space-based ISR system. First, there are assertions that the current intelligence cycle process can't handle the volume of data collected.[11] Second, "national" customers (e.g., non-military) complain that they can't get the data they need because the military is using up too much of the space-based ISR collection resources.[12] Lastly, military users complain that while they are getting lots of data, they aren't getting the information they need or want.[13] In sum, one group thinks there is too much data, another says there isn't enough, and a third says it doesn't matter because the data they do get isn't what they want anyway!

In the 1996-97 timeframe there were recommendations from congressional commissions and think tanks to merge NIMA, NRO and NSA as a way to solve the space-based ISR problems.[14] In addition, the Joint Staff has recently again asked if this option should be pursued. The "father" of reengineering, Dr. Michael Hammer, would advise that the "problems facing companies [or government organizations] do not result from their *organizational* structures, but from their *process* structures. (Emphasis in the original.)"[15] In other words, the reengineering recommendation would be to analyze the root of the problem you are trying to solve, scrutinize your business process to see what impact the root cause is having on your process, and look at current and near-term technologies to see if they can help do business in a better way. Only after doing these steps is it appropriate to overlay new structure.

Problem Statement

The question becomes, what is causing our current problems associated with space-based ISR and what fixes can we make? While the question is simple, the issues are extremely complex and tangled. In an effort to avoid the detailed entanglements and classification issues, the concepts discussed will be at a top-level or broad viewpoint.

4

This approach may be subject to criticism of being an "oversimplification" of the issues, but that is exactly what the author is trying to do—simplify the issues in order to get to the root problems relative to space-based ISR.

Our military customer has figured out what it wants from NIMA, NRO and NSA as evidenced by a speech given by General Myers, the Vice Chairman JCS, to the Defense Intelligence Agency (DIA) on 18 September 2000. "The new *Joint Vision 2020* takes the best parts of *Joint Vision 2010* and adds the key elements of knowledge and decision superiority. Basically it recognizes that future battlespace victory belongs to those who can *turn data into information, information into knowledge*, and *knowledge into superior battlespace decisions*. (Emphasis added.)"[16] The above quote uses some key language to help define just what it is that the military customer is looking for. To paraphrase the DoD Dictionary, "information" is data and fact that has been put into a context to provide meaning.[17] While this definition is helpful, we are lacking an official DOD definition for the term "knowledge." For this definition we can turn to one of the core determinations from the 1996 *Air Force 2025* study that defined knowledge of others as the sum of the informational components of knowing an adversary's intentions, plus their capabilities and their actions.[18] As further support for this determination, one of the cornerstone documents for the USIC, Executive Order 12333 identifies a very similar concept. "Timely and accurate information about the *activities, capabilities*, plans and *intentions* of foreign powers, organizations, and persons and their agents, is essential to the national security of the United States. All reasonable and lawful means must be used to ensure that the United States will receive the best intelligence available. (Emphasis added.)"[19]

This paper will present two points. First from a brief review of history a case can be made for equating the informational component of *intentions* with *intelligence*, *capabilities* with *reconnaissance* and *actions* with *surveillance*. What is key about this categorization is that it points out that we are currently missing a critical collection tool from the space-based ISR tool kit—a space-based *surveillance* system that could provide data concerning the *actions* of our adversary's on an on-demand basis. Without this third informational component, we will continue to come up short in the knowledge equation supporting information superiority.

This second point presented is that the intelligence cycle process in use today is from a period where intelligence was used as a preparatory step. Today, perhaps due to the availability of actions information in our everyday lives thanks to television and the Internet, we are now demanding that the intelligence cycle process increase its speed to provide a "response" capability in addition to its preparatory nature. However, the space-based ISR tools at our disposal for collecting information aren't really capable of capturing actions and thus the intelligence analysis cycle is having trouble meeting the informational demands of today's fast paced environment that wants to know what is happening—not just what has happened.

While a case can perhaps be made for gains in efficiencies with a structural merger of NIMA, NRO and NSA, the root of the current issues aren't structural. The current lack of a space-based surveillance system to provide actions data, and the incessant demand for that type of data from assets and a system incapable of providing it, is *a*, if not *the*, prime source of today's ISR problems for the US military customer.

Notes

[1] Joint Staff, Director for Strategic Plans and Policy, J-5, *Joint Vision 2020* (Washington D.C.: Government Printing Office, June 2000), 3-13.

[2] *Joint Vision 2020*, 8.

[3] *Joint Vision 2020*, 12.

[4] *Joint Vision 2020*, 10.

[5] National Commission for the Review of the National Reconnaissance Office (NRO Commission), *The NRO at the Crossroads*, 1 November 2000, on-line, 11; Internet, 29 November 2000, available from http://www.nrocommission.com.

[6] Air Force 2025, Air University, USAF Chief of Staff-directed futures study aimed at identifying the concepts, capabilities, and technologies the United States will require to remain the dominant air and space force in the 21st century, staff study, "Executive Summary," August 1996, 18.

[7] Jeffrey R. Cooper, "Strategy," in *Air and Space Power in the New Millennium,* ed. Daniel Goure' and Christopher M. Szara (Washington D.C.: Center for Strategic and International Studies, 1997), 75.

[8] Bruce D. Berkowitz and Allan E. Goodman, *Best Truth: Intelligence in the Information Age* (New Haven, Conn.: Yale University Press, 2000), 25; and Craig Covault, "NIMA Infotech Retools U.S. Space Recon Ops," *Aviation Week and Space Technology*, 7 August 2000, 63.

[9] Kevin C. Ruffner, ed., *CORONA: America's First Satellite Program* (Washington D.C.: History Staff, Center for the Study of Intelligence, Central Intelligence Agency, 1995), 11-14.

[10] Robert A. McDonald, "NRO's Satellite Imaging Reconnaissance: Moving from the Cold War Threat to Post-Cold War Challenges," *Defense Intelligence Journal: IMINT* 8, no. 1 (Summer 1999): 75; and NRO Commission, 21.

[11] Eric Schmitt, "Mapping Unit Failures Laid to Reorganization," *New York Times*, 12 May 1999, and Warren Ferster, "Lawmakers Warn of Reconnaissance Conflicts," *Defense News*, 23 October 2000.

[12] Walter Pincus, "Competition for Data From Satellites Rises," *Washington Post*, 20 November 2000.

[13] Vernon Loeb, "A Higher IQ Before the Marines Land," *Washington Post*, 17 November 2000 and "Interview U.S. Sen. Wayne Allard Comments on Space, Intell," *Space News*, 16 October 2000.

[14] House Permanent Select Committee on Intelligence, *IC 21: Intelligence Community in the 21st Century*, 104th Cong., (Washington, D.C.: Government Printing Office, 9 April 1996), I-17-19; on-line, Internet, 31 August 2000, available from http://www.access.gpo.gov/congress/house/intel/ic21/ic21_cov.html.

[15] Michael Hammer and James Champy, *Reengineering the Corporation: A Manifesto for Business Revolution* (New York, N.Y.: Harper Collins Publishers, Inc.,1994), 48.

[16] Gen Richard B. Myers, USAF, vice chairman joint chiefs of staff, address to the Defense Intelligence Agency, Washington D.C., 18 September 2000, 8.

Notes

[17] Joint Staff, Joint Doctrine Division, J-7, *Joint Publication 1-02, DOD Dictionary of Military Terms*; on-line, Internet, 13 November 2000, available from http://www.dtic.mil/doctrine/jel/doddict/data/i/03085.html.

[18] Air Force 2025, 41.

[19] Executive Order 12333, United States intelligence activities, 4 December 1981; on-line, Internet, 25 September 2000, available from http://www.nara.gov/fedreg/codific/eos/ e12333.html.

Chapter 2

Three Waves of Intelligence

The longer you look back, the farther you can look forward.

—Sir Winston Churchill

Pick-up almost any article on the US military today and you will see a reference to the need for, problems with, and/or the uses of ISR. Since the Gulf War, this acronym has become a well-worn abbreviation almost taking on a life of its own. Before that fully happens we need to revisit the term and ensure we understand what it really means and what the letters and words that comprise it really stand for.

To begin, the letter "I" in the acronym ISR is most often thought to represent the word *intelligence*. The letter "R" stands for *reconnaissance* and the letter "S" for *surveillance*. Typically the hierarchy of these terms is thought of as a pyramid with intelligence at its peak and with "S" and "R" depicted as sub-terms underneath feeding data to "I."

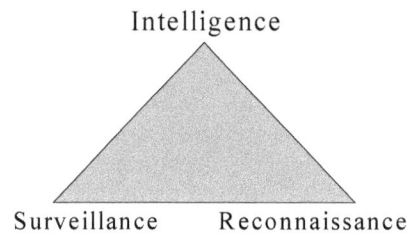

Figure 1 ISR Pyramid

Per the Department of Defense (DOD) Dictionary, the terms intelligence, reconnaissance and surveillance are defined as follows:

> Intelligence: 1. The product resulting from the collection, processing, integration, analysis, evaluation and interpretation of available information [facts, data, or instructions] concerning foreign countries or areas. 2. Information or knowledge about an adversary obtained through observation, investigation, analysis or understanding.[1]

> Reconnaissance: A mission undertaken to obtain by, visual observation or other detection methods, information about the activities and resources of an enemy or potential enemy, or to secure data concerning the meteorological, hydrographic or geographic characteristics of a particular area.[2]

> And,

> Surveillance: The systematic observation of aerospace, surface or subsurface areas, places, persons or things, by visual, aural, electronic, photographic or other means.[3]

This reveals a hodgepodge of definitional types that makes it very hard to understand what ISR is suppose to be. For instance, the first term, intelligence, is described as a product. The second term, reconnaissance is a mission, and the third term surveillance is an action. There is no common basis across the terms. Perhaps the most disconcerting problem is that the differences between surveillance and reconnaissance are never fully explained, and in some circles the terms are used interchangeably.[4] Both definitions include the verb "observation," and there is no difference between the two terms concerning their means, methods or target. It is easy to see why there might be miscommunication and confusion in the usage of the term ISR.

This chapter contends that there are distinct and important differences between intelligence, reconnaissance and surveillance that have either always been there, or are now coming to the surface due to the change in our decision making environment since the Gulf War. The three letters "I," "R" and "S" are actually co-equal terms that represent three separate and distinct data or informational categories. The last letter "S" represents a new data type that is even changing the way we use information. The story of "I", the story of "R," and the story of "S" will be used to make this case.

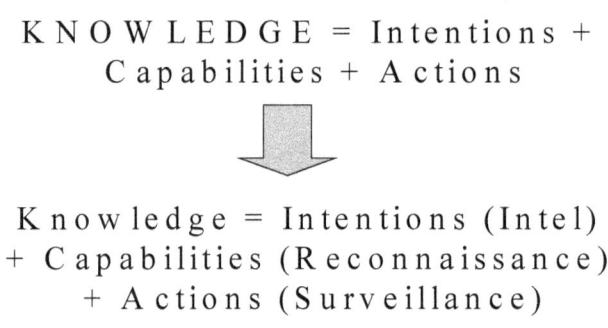

Figure 2 Knowledge Equals ISR

The Story of "I"

From early history we know that the word intelligence was used almost as a synonym for the finding out of an adversary's intentions. Former Director of Central Intelligence William Colby defined the "traditional concept of intelligence" as a "secret service which ferrets out an enemy's secret plan and shares it with a monarch so that he can win a battle."[5] Also from history we know that the first spying mechanism was a human whose purpose was to infiltrate an adversary's camp, either covertly or overtly, in order to learn the potential adversary's thoughts.[6] As technology progressed, physical presence within the range of a person's voice was no longer the only means by which to know what an adversary was planning to do. The technological achievement of writing opened up a whole new vista available for exploitation—the interception of an adversary's communiqués, today known as communications intelligence or COMINT.[7] One of the first documented cases of such an organized intelligence effort to learn the intentions of others was the interception and the deciphering of the coded letters from Mary Queen of Scots.

In the 1580's the Catholic Scottish queen was in a struggle for power with her Protestant English cousin, Elizabeth I. Mary and her conspirators had plans to overthrow Elizabeth in an effort to make England Catholic again. Unfortunately for Mary, Elizabeth's court contained a gentleman named Sir Francis Walsingham who had a great appreciation for spies and code breaking. Perhaps most unfortunate for Mary was the fact that Walsingham had formed an organized intelligence effort and had employed a preeminent code breaker by the name of Thomas Phelippes. Mary and her accomplices made the mistake of believing that their enciphering system was unbreakable even if their letters were somehow intercepted. The English intelligence effort triumph was the breaking of Mary's code and the presentation of her written treasonous intentions to the English court. This resulted in the beheading of Mary on February 8, 1587 in the Great Hall of Fotheringhay Castle and the protection of the reigning British monarch.[8] The value of an organized and technically capable "I" force was dramatically demonstrated.

The growth of an organized and technical intelligence service in the employ of nation states to infiltrate and intercept communications by countries in order to learn the intentions of their potential adversaries was commonplace in the 18th Century.

> By the 1700s cryptanalysis was becoming industrialized, with teams of government cryptanalysts working together to crack many of the most complex monoalphabetic ciphers. Each European power had its own so-called Black Chamber, a nerve center for deciphering messages and

gathering intelligence. The most celebrated, disciplined and efficient Black Chamber was the Geheime Kabinets-Kanzlei in Vienna. It operated according to a rigorous timetable, because it was vital that its nefarious activities should not interrupt the smooth running of the postal service. Letters which were supposed to be delivered to embassies in Vienna were first routed via the Black Chamber, arriving at 7 a.m. Secretaries melted seals, and a team of stenographers worked in parallel to make copies of the letters. If necessary, a language specialist would take responsibility for duplicating unusual scripts. Within three hours the letters had been resealed in their envelopes and returned to the central post office, so that they could be delivered to their intended destination. . . . Each day a hundred letters would filter through the Viennese Black Chamber.[9]

As man's communication technology has progressed, so has the technology for capturing, deciphering and translating intentions data. With the invention of the radio and telephony, the couriers that were targeted became the radio waves and communication wires in order to obtain the desired data. With each change in communication technology, new technical hurdles related to data access and volume had to be overcome.

> The biggest problem for cryptanalysis [in World War I] was dealing with the sheer volume of traffic. Before the advent of radio, intercepted messages were rare and precious items, and cryptanalysts cherished each one. However, in the First World War, the amount of radio traffic was enormous, and every single message could be intercepted, generating a steady flow of ciphertexts to occupy the minds of cryptanalysts. It is estimated that the French intercepted a hundred million words of German communications during the course of the Great War.[10]

A highpoint in the ability to capture and "break" adversary communications was achieved by the US in the 1940's as evidence by the histories made public regarding the German ENIGMA and the Japanese PURPLE code breaking efforts. "Through the end of World War II, COMINT (combined with cryptanalysis-the breaking of the codes and ciphers in which the valuable messages are transmitted) was more important than any other source of intelligence for the major powers, both in peace and in war. . . . Whatever its earlier successes, it is World War II that marks the heyday of British, as well as American, communications intelligence."[11]

Much of our nation's intention gathering successes since the end of World War II are still classified. We have been given a glimpse of early Cold War efforts with the declassification of the VENONA project and its communication intercepts and code breaking efforts that alerted US to the Soviet atomic weapon development and espionage efforts, but other efforts are still veiled in secrecy.[12] Nevertheless, today, whether we are talking about intercepting communications radio wave emanations to photons transiting fiber, at the very end of the 20th Century, the term "intelligence" is still used in a context that implies that "the primary intelligence challenge is to discern the adversary's interests and priorities."[13] In other words, the term intelligence today remains synonymous with the discerning of an adversary's intentions.

The Story of "R"

At some point in history, probably just after being startled by the learning of an adversary's intention, the need to determine whether an adversary had the capabilities to carry out their plans became a priority. An adversary's capabilities were probably first learned in early history by the human spy reconnoitering an area. Undoubtedly this task started off as an "on-foot" endeavor snooping around enemy territory and eventually evolved into an action that was done by the cavalry.[14] The task was to find out the details of enemy troop strength, levels of training, tactics, weapon types, number of weapons, and location of forces, as well as the capabilities of the terrain. With the advancement of industrial technology in the late 1800's and early 1900's, the spies and the horses were either supplemented or supplanted by mechanized ground vehicles, observation balloons, or airplanes.

Early attempts to perform aerial reconnaissance were demonstrated by the French in 1794 using manned balloons.[15] Prior to the invention of the readily transportable camera in the late 1820s, the spy (whether on foot, on a horse, or on some mechanical device) would make a mental picture, pen a note, or draw a sketch to depict what had been seen.[16] The camera was married to a US military aircraft for the first time in January 1911 to and "by the eve of World War I airplanes had so established themselves in reconnaissance, an activity traditionally undertaken by cavalry, that air units were even given cavalry names: squadrons."[17] The airplane's stature continued to improve during the war as it performed this critical data gathering role.

> Aerial reconnaissance had assumed mammoth proportions by the autumn of 1918. During the Meuse-Argonne offensive that September, for example, fifty-six thousand aerial reconnaissance prints were delivered to various U.S. Army units within a four-day period. The total number of prints produced between July 1, 1918, and Armistice Day the following November 11 came to 1.3 million, according to the United States Air Force's official account. "Toward the closing months of the war aerial photographs were handled so efficiently that many cases were recorded where only twenty minutes elapsed from the time an important photograph of enemy territory was taken until it had been brought to grounds developed, printed, interpreted and used as a basis for giving American batteries the proper range for artillery fire."[18]

Just as some called World War II the "heyday" of British and US COMINT activities, in other sources, aerial reconnaissance was identified as "the greatest single means of providing information of the enemy and the objectives in his territory."[19]

> Military applications of aerial photography expanded during World War II and many technological improvements in aircraft, camera and films followed. . . . Photo interpretation during World War II evolved into an exacting skill. Practitioners could extract important information from pictures that to the untrained eye appeared utterly meaningless. Most photo interpreters specialized in a particular piece of geography, weapons

system, type of engineering, and so forth, and the best of them eventually got to know their area so well that they became intuitive. They could look at a photograph taken straight down from an altitude of forty thousand feet, for example, and know instinctively that something had changed: that a power line had been added or a small ship moved, or a V-1 "Buzz-Bomb" was posed [*sic*] for firing.[20]

This was the real beginning of the rise of reconnaissance. Just as it took organization and technical skills to begin the rise of "I" back in the 18th Century, so it took the advent of the airplane and the camera to collect data on enemy capabilities and the development of a recognizable technical skill to exploit the data to cause the creation of a whole new being within the so-called *intelligence community*. This newly recognized intelligence discipline and its distinct "capability data" product became vital during the Cold War as the primary means of collecting information behind the Iron Curtain. The ever-increasing need for this new type of data resulted in development of the first ever aircraft, the U-2, whose sole purpose was as a reconnaissance platform.[21] (Prior to the U-2, aerial reconnaissance had been viewed as an "additional duty" and was performed by fighters or bombers that had been modified to fill this role.[22])

The benefits of adding "capability data" to the intelligence analysis process was a great boon to our national leaders in the 1960s. "Where before, in the 1950s, Eisenhower administration officials worked with virtually no reliable intelligence information on Soviet military preparations and capabilities [from spies and COMINT sources], their successors by the late 1960s dealt with a surfeit of such information [from overhead reconnaissance], almost all of it totally reliable."[23] "Miles Copeland, an intelligence officer who served with Allen Dulles in the OSS during World War II and retired from the CIA considered the marked change [in our ability to collect information] and reflected, 'a satellite circling the world . . . will pick up more information in a day than the espionage service could pick up in a year.' Bespeaking the significance of this revolution, a few years after Eisenhower left office, President Lyndon Johnson publicly described robotic space reconnaissance as the most important and valuable of all American astronautical activities."[24]

At that point in time, President Johnson was correct; but, then things changed due to the ready availability of nuclear weapons and their rapid delivery systems poised for launch. Timelines for analysis of "intentions data" and "capability data" shrunk; and it became important to know more than what the enemy intended to do, or what they were capable of doing. It became of vital national importance to know directly what the enemy was doing.

The Rise of "S"

In a military context, information concerning an adversary's real-time actions has always been the hardest information to attain prior to a battle being joined. It has always been desired to be able to observe the actions of one's adversary prior to the start of physical violence so as to facilitate the out-maneuvering of the opponent and bring the other war principles of surprise, mass and economy of force all to bear. In the past, this was not possible due to technical limitations that limited the depth of one's view into enemy territory and/or the inability to reliably communicate information concerning adversary actions back to the battle commander with enough speed so the information didn't revert to being a historic account of what had happened instead of a real-time report of what was happening. It takes three components to constitute surveillance as illustrated by the US Civil War account below.

When Signalman Captain Alexander wigwagged a warning to Colonel "Shanks" Evans on Sunday, July 26,1861, his message spoiled General McDowell's scheme to encircle the Confederate army, dashing hopes that Bull Run would be the first and only major conflict in a civil war. The warning that Union infantry and artillery "could turn his flank" was succinct, precise, and, above all else, timely. Battlefield geometry at Manassas helped: *The sensor, the sensed, and the command and control node were all within eyesight of one another.* General Beauregard immediately shifted his forces, changing the outcome of this battle and the course of the Civil War. (Emphasis added)[25]

In order to be surveillance, it is critical for the collection system, the target, and the decision maker to be in contact with each other in such a way that the *actions* of the enemy are relayed in real-time to those who can make decisions to counter the enemy actions. This is perhaps the key insight to the real discriminator between the two terms. Typically time, or the size of area covered, has been used as the primary basis of differentiation between reconnaissance and surveillance in the past; but, these distinctions have always seemed hollow and not really accurate due to actual data collection practices. The reason for time and area of coverage not being good discriminators is because they are resultants of the difference—not the cause. The key difference between the two terms is their purpose.

As explained previously, the purpose of reconnaissance is to provide data on the *capabilities* of an adversary or of terrain. Reconnaissance can provide location of things, features of things, number of things, and the results of what happened. The very nature of a photograph denotes the data it depicts as history. In contrast, the purpose of surveillance is to observe and report on what is happening in real-time. "Happenings" are moving events or *actions*, thus the purpose of surveillance is to report on the *actions* of things in the present tense. Actions can't be captured in a picture—its takes multiple frames of images to do that. An illustrative example to further depict the difference between reconnaissance and surveillance is the story concerning the Soviet bomber and missile gaps that resulted in the first space-based surveillance system.

The "Gap" Story

From the open press it appears we first learned of the Soviet's intentions and efforts to develop atomic weapons through our spies and COMINT efforts, the most famous to date being the recently declassified VENONA program which described the Soviet HUMINT efforts to steal our atomic bomb technological secrets.[26] Shortly after the VENONA discoveries in 1947, the US began reconnoitering the Soviet Union using balloons for over flight and aircraft flying about its periphery trying to gather evidence for signs that the Soviets had the capability to detonate an atomic bomb.[27] Once that fact was verified, next came the efforts to determine if the Soviets had the capabilities to deliver their new weapon in large numbers, thus determining the actual numbers of Soviet bombers and missiles became a concern. "Fears of a Soviet surprise nuclear attack affected not just Western leaders. A poll conducted in the mid 1950s indicated that more than half of all American citizens thought that they were more likely to die in a nuclear attack than from old age."[28] In order to determine whether or not the Soviets had these capabilities, President Eisenhower in the late 1950s and early 1960s authorized the U-2 spy plane and CORONA satellites to be built in order to conduct reconnaissance to gather the needed data on Soviet nuclear weapon delivery capabilities.[29] This was necessary in order to supplement and confirm the previously mentioned intentions data we had gotten through our spying and COMINT efforts.[30]

These new overhead photo reconnaissance systems confirmed that the Soviets did indeed have a bomber and missile delivery system capable of delivering their atomic weapons, but the photos also showed that the numbers of bombers and missiles were few. While that was the good news, as early as 1956, the CIA had warned that it was possible for the Soviet Union to conduct a surprise nuclear attack on the U.S. "without undertaking any observable preparations that could provide strategic warning."[31] The only type of assets we had available to us at that time were "I" assets and "R" assets which required analysis and interpretation in order to generate projections of adversary actions.

In the past we had been content with only having intentions data and capability data for three reasons. First, we could collect this type of data typically without committing an act of war (violation of a nation's sovereignty). Second, we had built an analytical apparatus geared to effectively exploit the "I" and "R" data in order to derive an adversary's potential courses of actions in a timely enough manner to allow us to develop and take counter actions at the same or faster rate of the adversary. Third, we either had enough resources so we could afford to develop multiple counter-actions, or the consequences of guessing wrong were not devastating. As long as the time factors for deriving potential actions, and the consequences of analytical mistakes concerning the projection of enemy actions were acceptable, there was no problem with relying on "I" and "R" data.

But reliance on "I" and "R" systems changed with the advent of atomic weapons and inter-continental ballistic missiles. The nation could no longer afford to rely solely on "I" and "R" data types. The analysis time would have taken too long and the consequences of guessing wrong might have meant the destruction of the country. This new situation drove the need for a system to directly observe the Soviet missile fields. A system that could provide incontrovertible proof of Soviet launch actions in a timely manner became a national priority. The system initially resulted in the building of ground based radars that could detect incoming Soviet bombers and missiles so we could retaliate, but it also meant the creation of a space-based surveillance system designed to detect the Soviet *actions* of launching their missiles that became known in the 1970s as the Defense Support Program (DSP).[32] The DSP was all about watching the actions of the adversary so we would know how to properly respond. This was the beginning of the rise of space-based surveillance.

Wrong Tools for the Job

As already covered, we have been technically limited in the past to perform surveillance of action behind an adversary's borders. Beyond the specific application for missile launch detection that DSP provides, we still are lacking in the ability to observe physical actions and movements via a "deep-look" surveillance prior to hostilities being declared. What is in some ways staggering, is that our ability to perform surveillance of enemy territory has only improved by a distance of approximately 100 miles from the time of Napoleon when he used balloons to increase the depth and breadth of his view.[33]

In the Gulf War, we were able to use marvelous surveillance capabilities such as the DSP missile detection satellites and the Joint Surveillance and Target Attack Radar System (JSTARS) and Airborne Warning and Control System (AWACS) aircrafts to monitor and report on enemy ground and air actions to give our field commanders a real-time representation of the battlespace like no general in history had ever really had before.[34] However, those airborne surveillance systems were still constrained at the beginning of the crisis by the political environment, and later by the operational threat

21

environment that dictated how deep they could look. Even so, the "information technology unveiled in the Persian Gulf war gave combat forces a tantalizing glimpse of what commanders have hungered for since the dawn of human conflict: A 'God's Eye' view of the battlefield, providing the same comprehensive and real-time perspective of battle given to those generals who once commanded from horseback and hill top."[35]

In addition to these surveillance systems, the military was provided high priority access to imaging reconnaissance satellites. Ever since this access was provided there have been cries from the non-military customers of the US IC that the space-based imaging reconnaissance resources have been used up by the military and that the analysis arm of the IC can't keep up with the volume of images collected. There was no "tasking" problem with the U-2 or CORONA in the 1960s and today we have more capability on orbit than we had then. Why wasn't there a problem then and why is there a problem now? The reason is that the value of surveillance has been dramatically proven in battle.

> Proof of value [of surveillance] was demonstrated by the fact that aircraft directed by Joint STARS had a 90 percent success rate in finding targets on the first pass. In one incident, according to Colonel Muellner, two A-10s and an AC-130 directed by Joint STARS destroyed fifty-eight of sixty-one vehicles in a single convoy. On another occasion a unit forming to attack VII Corps was 80 percent disabled before it could get into action. . . . Air Force Chief of Staff General Merrill McPeak said: "We will never again want to fight a war without a Joint STARS kind of system."[36]

Prior to this event, real-time reporting on enemy actions behind their lines was desired, but not expected. Today it is demanded. This is probably due in no small way to the shrinkage of the well known observe, orient, decide act (OODA) decision timeline. Previous research has shown that during the Revolutionary War, observation took 24 hours, orientation took 14 days, deciding took 30 days, and acting was spread out over a

60 day period. During the Civil War, observation took 12 hours, orientation took 3 days, decisions took 14 days and actions spanned a 30-day period. In World War II, observation took 3 hours, orientation took 30 minutes, decisions were made over 3 days and actions took 7. Lastly in Desert Storm, observations took 45 seconds, orientation was cut to 10 minutes, decisions were made over 8 hours and actions spanned 1 day.[37]

Table 1 OODA Loop Shrinkage

	Revolutionary War	Civil War	WW II	Gulf War	War of Tomorrow
Observe	24 hrs	12 hours	3 hours	45 seconds	Continuous
Orient	14 days	3 days	30 minutes	10 minutes	Continuous
Decide	30 days	14 days	3 days	8 hours	Immediate
Act	60 days	30 days	7 days	1 day	Hours

This kind of decision time shrinkage is what caused the creation of the DSP surveillance system for detection of nuclear missile a launch actions. It appears to also be working again, but for conventional conflict this time.

It is a fact that the current on-orbit imaging systems are designed for reconnaissance and not of surveillance.[38] This point is either immaterial or not understood by those that are asking for surveillance due to the overwhelming need for the actions data on our adversaries and/or due to our analytic community's history of being able to provide information concerning projected enemy actions from pieces of static data. In the photographic reconnaissance business it is called "comparative coverage" and "remains a cornerstone of imaging analysis."[39] It involves "comparing pictures of the same target that were taken on successive days or weeks in order to spot such changes as troops buildups or withdrawals, bridge or road construction, armament stockpiling, the laying of railroad tracks."[40] What is interesting about this example is the taking of a picture to see where the enemy is located, how much material his has, and the status of his logistical system are all valid reconnaissance tasks that are trying to determine the *capabilities* of the enemy. It is even a valid reconnaissance task to see if an adversary's capability has changed. But the moment the customer need to know the rate of the adversary's capability change and/or what his activities are, then the purpose of the data collection act isn't trying to determine capabilities anymore, it is trying to determine action, and the purpose of the task has transitioned from reconnaissance to surveillance. [While much of the discussion relative to "R" has been focused on imagery in order to simplify the discussion, in truth, electronic intelligence (ELINT), foreign instrumentation signals intelligence (FISINT) and measures and signatures intelligence (MASINT) can also be considered intelligence types primarily focused on determining the "capabilities" of the target. Actions that are occurring are derived from the analysis of the ELINT, FISINT and MASINT data much like comparative imagery analysis.]

Since the rise of reconnaissance we have been compensating with analytical expertise for the lack of our ability to loiter and surveil. We have in essence been using screwdrivers to pound in nails. It can be done, but it is not the way it should be done. The best analogy may be supplied by comparing a camcorder and a 35mm camera.

If you want to capture the action of your child hitting a baseball, the best tool is probably a camcorder. If you just want a picture of your child with a baseball bat, use a camera. Problems arise when you really want to capture actions, but don't have a camcorder. You could use the 35mm in a fast shutter mode to snap a lot of pictures of your child swinging at the ball in an attempt to capture pieces of the act, but this would be a very inefficient use of the still picture camera.

This is exactly what is happening today as evidenced by a review of the satellite imaging tasking for Operation ALLIED FORCE over Kosovo. Specifically the image tasking for the period of 24 Mar 99 through 24 May 99 was reviewed and categorized by the author. The result of the analysis showed that 50% of all priority imaging requests for our nation's classified space-based imaging constellation was for surveillance of targets within the Kosovo area explicitly asking for a monitoring of movements and adversary actions.[41] (A percentage has to be used here due the classification of the actual total number of requests that might indicate to an adversary the nature of our actual capacities.) We are trying to use 35mm cameras in the form of imaging spy satellites to capture adversary actions. We are then flooding the analysts with these pictures and asking for a rapid analysis of what is happening from a group that has been trained to be methodical and systematic in the extraction of data that is within the picture.

The military is using space-based reconnaissance tools in this way because of the need to know what is happening and because they are the only tools with the appropriate deep-look view afforded from space right now. In other words, the military user will use the 35mm camera because he can't wait on the camcorder to be provided, and isn't being directly charged for development of the film.

The military user has gotten a taste for how powerful surveillance can be to mission accomplishment and understands the view afforded by space-based sensors. With the customer demand readily apparent and the technical ability apparently within reach, the solution to the current ISR problem is to tackle the root cause and develop this new tool. In the mean time, pressure will continue to be brought to bear on the current information generation process to produce information it is not capable of providing in an accurate and timely manner.

Notes

[1] Joint Staff, Joint Doctrine Division, J-7, *Joint Publication 1-02, DOD Dictionary of Military Terms*; on-line, Internet, 13 November 2000, available from http://www.dtic.mil/doctrine/jel/doddict/data/i/03160.html.

[2] DOD Dictionary, http://www.dtic.mil/doctrine/jel/doddict/data/r/05189.html.

[3] DOD Dictionary, http://www.dtic.mil/doctrine/jel/doddict/data/s/06128.html.

[4] Maj James P. Marshall, USAF "Near Real-Time Intelligence of the Tactical Battlefield," in *Theater Air Campaign Studies*, ed. Maj Pat Battles (Maxwell AFB, Ala.: Air University Press, 1995), 231.

[5] Abram N. Shulsky and Gary J. Schmitt, *Silent Warfare: Understanding the World of Intelligence*, 2nd ed. (New York N.Y.: Macmillan Publishing Company, 1993), 179.

[6] Shulsky, 179.

[7] DOD Dictionary, http://www.dtic.mil/doctrine/jel/doddict/data/c/01390.html

[8] Simon Singh, *The Code Book* (New York, N.Y.: Random House Inc., 1999) 32-43.

[9] Singh, 59.

[10] Singh, 104.

[11] Shulsky, 29-30.

[12] Lt Gen Michael V. Hayden, USAF, Director, National Security Agency, address to Kennedy Political Union of American University, Washington D.C., 17 February 2000, 2.

[13] RAND, *Project Air Force: 1999 Annual Report*, 34.

[14] Capt David H. Foglesong, USAF, "Intelligence, Dominant Battlespace Knowledge, and the Warfighter" (masters thesis, Joint Military Intelligence College, August 1998), 11.

[15] William E. Burrows, *Deep Black* (New York, N.Y.: Random House Inc., 1986), 28-30, and Jim Mohan, "Tracing NIMA's Roots," 15 September 2000, 4, and *Encyclopedia Britannica*, s.v. "balloon," on-line, Internet, 6 November 2000, available from http://www.britannica.com/bcom/eb/article/1/0,5716,12171,+1+12019,00. html.

[16] Burrows, 28-29.

[17] Burrows, 32.

[18] Burrows, 35.

[19] Maj Dana G. Richard, USAFR, "United States Joint Intelligence in World War II—Its Organization and Effectiveness as Determined by Its Contribution to Allied Information Superiority" (masters thesis, Joint Military Intelligence College, August 1999), 23.

[20] Mohan, 12.

[21] R. Cargill Hall, "Postwar Strategic Reconnaissance and the Genesis of CORONA," in *Eye in the Sky: The Story of the CORONA Spy Satellites*, ed. Dwayne A. Day, John M. Logsdon and Brian Latell (Washington D.C.: Smithsonian Institution Press, August 1999), 97-101.

[22] Hall, CORONA, 97-101.

Notes

[23] Hall, Eisenhower, 68.

[24] Hall, Eisenhower, 68.

[25] Alan D. Camden, "Communications Support to Intelligence," in *The First Information War*, ed. Alan D. Camden (Fairfax, V.A.: AFCEA International Press, October 1992), 51.

[26] Hayden, address.

[27] Hayden address; and Curtis Peebles, *High Frontier: The U.S. Air Force and the Military Space Program* (Washington, D.C.: Government Printing Office, 1997), 2.

[28] Peebles, 3.

[29] John L. McLucas, address to the Air Force Historical Foundation Symposium, Andrews AFB, MD, 21-22 September 1995, "The U.S. Space Program Since 1961." in *The U.S. Air Force in Space, 1945 to the 21st Century*, ed., R. Cargill Hall and Jacob Neufeld (Washington, D.C.: Government Printing Office, 1998), 79-80.

[30] Hall, Eisenhower, 61.

[31] Peebles, 32.

[32] Peebles, 32-37.

[33] Maj Kimberly M. Corcoran, USAF, "Higher Eyes in the Sky: The Feasibility of Moving AWACS and JSTARS Functions into Space," (masters thesis, School of Advanced Air Power Studies, October 1999), 1.

[34] Camden, 51-53.

[35] Camden, 58.

[36] Thomas L. Swalm, "Joint STARS in Desert Storm," in *The First Information War*, ed. Alan D. Camden (Fairfax, V.A.: AFCEA International Press, October 1992), 169-170.

[37] CAPT Clarence E. Carter, USN, et al. "The Man in the Chair: Cornerstone of Global Battlespace Dominance," in *Air Force 2025, White Papers Volume 1: Awareness*, (Maxwell AFB, Ala.: Air University Press, September 1996), 194.

[38] Berkowitz, 35.

[39] Burrows, 35.

[40] Burrows, 35.

[41] Lt Col James O. Norman, Air Force Fellow, memorandum to NIMA/CITO, subject: Tasking Statistics for Use in Research Paper (U), 1 March 2001. (Secret/TK) Information extracted in unclassified.

Chapter 3

A New Information Process?

The Information Revolution is not just about cheaper communications or faster computers. The Information Revolution is also changing how people use information. As a result, organizations such as the intelligence community must change their modi operandi in order to provide it. The Information Revolution is bringing into question many of the basic principles about how intelligence is "supposed to work." To adapt, the intelligence community must abandon many of these principle replacing them with a new approach.

—Author Bruce D. Berkowitz

From the number of books and articles written on the subject, it appears that the intelligence cycle, the process by which the US IC generates its products, is under great pressure to change. One reason for this pressure may be due to the desires and demands of its military customers to know what is happening right now with any event of interest. In the past, this was not a problem due to lowered expectations of what an intelligence system could provide.[1] An example is recounted by former Vice Chairman JCS Admiral William Owens, "These were the realities of combat in the mid-1940s: primitive surveillance capabilities that generally failed to inform the commanders of battlefield events; fragile communications technology on which the commanders relied to direct the planned operation, and the age-old reliance on mass—overwhelming numbers of ships, aircraft, and soldiers—to compensate for the many unknowns of battle."[2] Intelligence was viewed as a tool of preparation, but today it is needed to be a tool of real-time response.

In the past, categories of intelligence were created to help sort out priorities and resources and show distinctions between intelligence gathering equipments and efforts. National-level intelligence focused on "national" issues such as learning the intentions of the other entity during diplomatic negotiations, discerning the capabilities of a new weapon system, or calculating the capability of the Soviet Union to feed its people from photos of its wheat crop. Strategic intelligence efforts were viewed as a focused subset of national intelligence concerned with nuclear targeting, the intentions of those that had the decision making power to launch a nuclear attacks, and the capabilities of those nuclear weapon systems. Tactical intelligence efforts were focused on conventional military items of interest and were typically a separate and distinct set of assets used to collect and analyze the information gathered for tactical military applications.

Today these old categories have become meaningless. "Despite Gulf War complaints about intelligence support, technology has made it possible to pass raw and finished intelligence rapidly down the line from national technical systems to local commanders. It has already blurred, if not eliminated, the distinction between national and tactical intelligence, and has made national intelligence highly relevant to tactical operations."[3] In other words, the systems that used to be private purview of national-level decision-makers have been made available to the military user.

The distinctions between categories of intelligence are no longer about the customer or the type of information desired. The difference is now how much time someone has to decide on a course of action for our country to take. This new distinction was first identified in the 1996 House Permanent Select Committee on Intelligence Staff Study known as *IC21: Intelligence Community in the 21st Century,* by describing the problem as "not a 'national versus military' dichotomy, but rather a near-term [response] or crisis focus at the expense of medium- to long-term [preparation] requirements. . . ."[4] The Independent Commission on the National Imagery and Mapping Agency, (AKA: NIMA Commission), in their December 2000 report echoed this previous finding, "The Commission finds that the issue is not one of national intelligence requirements versus tactical intelligence requirements, nor is it strategic versus tactical. Rather, the issue is one of balancing long-term intelligence support and analysis versus short-term (*i.e.,* crisis support) intelligence support and analysis."[5] The current space-based "I" and "R" tools were built for the prior era of providing data for preparation. Unfortunately, so is the current intelligence process that produces the information from the data collected.

The Current Process

The current in vogue Washington D.C. acronym that represents the US IC's intelligence cycle is "TPED" or "T[C]PED" which stands for Tasking, Collection, Processing, Exploitation and Dissemination.[6] This process is typically depicted in a serial manner either in a line or in a circle with one activity feeding into the next.

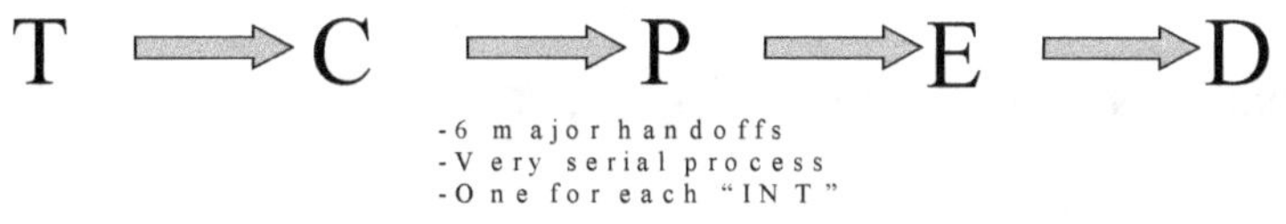

$$T \Rightarrow C \Rightarrow P \Rightarrow E \Rightarrow D$$

-6 major handoffs
-Very serial process
-One for each "INT"

Figure 3 Current IC Process

This is a minor variation from the process described in *Joint Pub 2-0* that lists Planning and Direction; Collection; Processing and Exploitation; Analysis and Production; and Dissemination and Integration as the intelligence cycle steps.[7] The Central Intelligence Agency's *Factbook on Intelligence* describes the intelligence cycle steps as Planning and Direction; Collection; Processing; All Source Analysis and Production; and Dissemination.[8] An interesting point is how similar, if not identical, the above descriptions are to the intelligence cycle steps of Direction, Collection, Collation, Evaluation, Interpretation and Dissemination used by US forces in World War II.[9] The point here is not the minor differences in each of these descriptions of the intelligence cycle.

Table 2 Intelligence Cycle Process Comparison

	Step 1	Step 2	Step 3	Step 4	Step 5
Current	Tasking	Collection	Processing	Exploitation	Dissemination
Joint Pub 2	Planning & Direction	Collection	Processing & Exploitation	Analysis & Production	Dissemination & Integration
CIA	Planning & Direction	Collection	Processing	Analysis & Production	Dissemination & Integration
WWII	Direction	Collection	Collation	Evaluation & Interpretation	Dissemination

The subtle nuances between the terms exploitation, analysis, and production, or the teasing apart of the boundaries between collection and processing or processing and exploitation are not important. "The intelligence cycle reflects the best thinking of how an information service should work from the late 1940s and 1950s, when people began to write about intelligence policy and develop concepts about how intelligence organizations ought to operate."[10] What is astonishing is that the intelligence cycle process, despite the advance of technology, has essentially remained the same for the US military and IC since World War II. For fifty years, no major change has occurred to the process of generating information. Certainly some steps have gotten faster and our ability to gather more bits has increased, but the essential sequence of events has remained unchanged.

The Old School—Knowledge versus Information

Most would agree that the US IC has a rich history and an overall successful story for the last half of the 20th Century. The foundations for the current US IC structure, just like the intelligence cycle process, were forged from the lessons learned during World War II.[11] One of the reasons given for the surprise attack on Pearl Harbor was a muddled, uncoordinated intelligence system that existed amongst the various entities that tried to do intelligence.[12] Thus an organizational fix was sought after the war in order to prevent such a surprise attack from ever occurring again. The best minds of the time were asked to construct a US IC, and they used a model with which they were most familiar.

> Picture the typical American college in the 1940s. This was the environment in which Sherman Kent, William Langer and many other founding fathers of the analytical side of the U.S. intelligence community first worked. It was also their reference point for how intelligence organizations ought to function to support policymakers. Look at a handful of college catalogues from the period and an interesting detail falls out: the way people measured the quality of a college or university at the time. Most of the prestigious institutions boasted about how many volumes—books, journals, and original papers their library held. (Harvard's library took honors with 5,274,618 volumes in 1949, making it the envy of other institutions.) At the time, libraries were literally storehouses of knowledge, just as, say, silos were storehouses of grain. So, the more knowledge, the better the institution. The same rule implicitly applied to the faculty. The best way to interact with someone was in a face-to-face conversation, so the quality of the college was linked to the number of knowledgeable faces one might encounter on campus. In

short, when the modern intelligence community was established and, with it, the basic framework for the agencies and departments that remain with us today—information was scarce, expensive, and considered authoritative when provided by organizations with accepted credentials.[13]

Perhaps because of its academic heritage, the analysis side of the US IC attitude seems to be that "analysis" is the "bedrock of intelligence" that provides knowledge and without analysis all that an organization has is raw data.[14] Books such as *Dominant Battlespace Knowledge* (DBK) run counter to this approach since their main tenet is for the operational decision maker to be able to receive information in real-time and instantly act upon it.[15]

A sense of frustration with today's high-speed information environment and customer demands for real-time information can be seen in some recent theses and papers sponsored by the Defense Intelligence Agency's Joint Military Intelligence College (JMIC) A 1996 Occasional Paper from JMIC tries to make the case that intelligence is more than information—that intelligence is actually synonymous with knowledge.[16] The essence of the IC's confusion is nicely captured in the following quote from a 1999 Defense Intelligence Agency Joint Military Intelligence College master's thesis, "Although identifying the role of intelligence in *information superiority* seems as though it should be a straightforward undertaking, it is in fact difficult. Intelligence is assumed to be a major component of *information superiority*, but the linkage is not clearly stated and good intelligence alone does not guarantee *information superiority*. . . .there is no prevailing framework within which to consider the role of intelligence."[17] Much like a stockbroker sees himself as the provider of advice based on knowledge and wisdom, so does today's intelligence analyst see this as his or her role.[18]

While it is true that an intelligence analyst may become knowledgeable on a particular topic, or region of the world, that's not the end goal. The IC might be able to supply people as advisers that are knowledgeable, but it cannot deliver knowledge. Knowledge has to reside within the decision maker, not just the advisor, or else the advisor becomes the real decider. Today's military consumer is not looking for decisions from the analyst. "It is the job of intelligence specialists to define facts, gaps in facts, and the logical conclusion of facts. . . . Expecting the intelligence community to provide summary judgments on unknowable events is a throwback to an older style of using information."[19]

As far as the military customer of ISR data is concerned, it isn't about knowledge provided by the analyst or the volume of analyzed information, "it's about getting the right information to the right person at the right time. It's about *decision* superiority, not intelligence superiority."[20] Decisions have to be made. They can't always wait for research and analysis to be coordinated, edited and formally supplied. Today's military customers are asking for accurate and timely information that helps them decide what is going on and what might occur. Summary judgments that have been coordinated through and provided by an institution aren't useful. The following excerpt from the Vice Chairman's recent speech make this point clear.

> Let me offer an up to the minute, real-world example I see every day wearing the Vice Chairman's hat. Every morning I get a stack of highly classified intelligence reports from a number of agencies. If, for example, Saddam Hussein shakes up his cabinet, the NSA, the CIA, the DIA and J2 all analyze the significance, and send me a pouch reporting essentially the same event—well after it happens. And as I go through these similar reports, I find myself hunting for the significant differences of opinion. It's often from *that* insight that I draw my own conclusions about the potential effect of the change. What I would really prefer is two-fold. First, on any given day, I would rather have a consolidated report on a

single event, along with a list of different opinions among the various experts on its significance. Second, while I want them to tell me what's important, I also want the ability to go in myself and get the specific information that I'm interested in—the information I need to make the right decision about how to respond. . . . On a different scale, but within the same framework, I'm certain that the war fighter would prefer the same thing. Everyone form the CINC to the soldier, sailor, airman or marine operating his weapon system would benefit.[21]

The New Use of Information

From our own everyday experiences we are now use to getting data about what is happening on events we care about and expect to get it when we ask for it. Initially we were trained to expect it by television. Visions of real-time CNN reporting from Baghdad at the start of the Gulf War come to mind. But undoubtedly the real change occurred due to the Internet and the growth of IT capabilities like real-time paging and e-mail alerts. Some observations about the impacts on society and the change in information usage are enlightening.

> The Information Revolution is not only about hardware and software, but also about behavior and culture. The explosion in information technology developments has changed how society and individuals use and interact with information. Specifically:
>
> -People have come to expect information on demand. They often prefer to be in direct contact with whatever sensor or human reporter is collecting information for them. If they cannot be in direct contact, they at least expect to know their information is being gathered so that they can assess its credibility and accuracy for themselves, and so that they can make adjustments.
>
> -"Channel surfing" is more than a cliché. It describes how people consume information today. In and age of media conglomerates, thousand-channel cable services, and the Internet, people usually have many sources of information from which to choose. Information consumers quickly change channels, switch stations, or cancel their cable service if they are dissatisfied with the quality of the support they receive or if they doubt its content.

-Partly because of the greater availability of information, and partly because of the general decline in deference to institutions, people are reluctant simply to accept "wisdom" from authority figures. People often prefer to evaluate data themselves, or have experts they trust do so on their behalf. Even at the highest levels, policymakers can now function as their own analyst in ways and at a depth that was not possible only a few years ago.[22]

These are powerful changes in the way we use and expect to use information. In a recent report from UCLA titled *Surveying the Digital Future*, noted that while some 19 million Americans were using the Internet in 1997, 100 million were using it in 1999.[23] A five-fold increase in usage in three years! The measure of a university is no longer just its books and resident scholars. "Today's top universities do not boast only about their libraries, but about their 'connectivity' and how their students can reach their professors and access the Internet without leaving their dorm rooms."[24] In fact, our information practices and capabilities in our home life are probably ahead of our professional military experiences. Case in point is the stock market.

Lessons To Be Learned?

The intelligence community and academia are not the only entities that are being affected by the IT enabled rise of surveillance, and the way consumers use information. A good comparison example is the financial investment industry, an entity that use to be a "private reserve" just like intelligence but is now open to millions. "An unprecedented 49% of American households today own stocks, either directly or through a mutual funds and 401(k) plans, compared with just 4% in 1952. . . . In the "Old Economy" days, the stock market was a source of stability. Wealthy old men would read the listings in the morning paper and learn that their shares had swung up ¼ or down 1/8. Today we have the Internet and the 'CNBC effect.' People see a trend as it's happening and call or click their broker to chase the momentum."[25] This "CNBC effect" that allows investors to see a trend as it is happening from their television set or their computer screen is surveillance. Perhaps a foretelling for the US IC is how this once stable commercial industry has had to adapt its process and structures.

Not too long ago stocks were traded by investors having to call their broker and discuss with him or her various investment and trading options. Usually the only information a private investor had was the data provided in monthly or weekly investment magazines like *Smart Money* and the *Kiplinger Letter*, or the daily *Wall Street Journal*. The broker, on the other hand, was privy to industry investment research reports and real-time stock market trends. Whether the broker was really able to use the large amount of data and information at his disposal was another matter, but since it wasn't available to the investor it was a moot point. Most people were exposed to the stock market ticker during the evening news after the markets were closed. The product of the investment firms was trading access, pieces of paper called "stocks," and the wealth it made for its investors because of the advice it gave to its customer based on its market research and judgment.

Today this situation has changed. While investment firms are still doing brokerage business, the growing or additional customer market is supporting the "day-trader" or personal investor. Access to trade is now available to anyone. Stocks are numbers on a computer screen, and the investors are responsible for generating their own wealth from the judgments and decisions they make. The selection of investment firms for these customers is based in large part on the timeliness, accuracy and relevance of the information they supply that enables the investor to make the right decision. These firms are now in the information business. An interesting story is one that comes from a DoD sponsored benchmark report concerning the conversion of what use to be a monthly investment magazine that did market research; but, is also now an on-line real-time stock market surveillance system and the impact it is having on the industry.

Smart Money

In 1997, the Dow Jones and Co. Inc. created a website that didn't just duplicate the *Smart Money* magazine in an electronic form, but instead added informational value for their customers. The company took advantage of the Internet medium to provide an information service no magazine ever could. It provided an ability to visually surveil the actions of the stock market without having to read or interpret letters or numbers. Data was put into context and converted into information immediately and in real time by using visual shapes and color. (To really get the point of this section, the reader is encouraged to go to the smartmoney.com website at http://www.smartmoney.com, click on the "Map of the Market" hyperlink, and then perform the actions described below.)

For instance, in the picture on the next page you will notice large block market segments of health care, finance, energy and so on. Within each large market sector block, smaller boxes represent the various companies within each sector. The company name associated with each block appears by simply moving your mouse over the "map." The color of the box indicates whether that companies stock is losing or making money with the intensity of the shade indicating the rate of change. In this example, red indicates that the stock price is currently down, green indicates that the stock price is up, and black represents an unchanged price. The size of the company box indicates its market share within the sector. By clicking on the company box, an investor can see the

38

numerical data showing the financial loss or gain and can also drill down several layers to access research reports on the company's history, plans (i.e., intentions), capacity, capabilities as well as similar information on their competitors.[26]

What is interesting is this industry had similar information analysis problems that the US IC faces today. They needed a way to share information with laymen that was quick and accurate but wouldn't swamp the user. They correctly deduced that visualization was the key to being able to organize and present the volumes of action data, due to a human's greatest capacity to process information being in the visual realm (i.e., billions of bits per second) versus auditory (i.e., tens of thousands of bits per second) or oral (i.e., 50 bits per second) presentation formats.[27]

By paying for a subscription to the website, the investor is allowed to see a Map of the Market that is being updated in near-real time (seconds worth of data transmission and processing delays) and thus monitor entire industry segment market actions as they are happening. Even though subscriptions to the magazine are double the number of real-time subscribers to the web site (i.e., the magazine has roughly on million subscribers to approximately five hundred thousand for the web site), in some ways the *Smart Money* magazine is now a supplement the website by responding to educated consumer e-mails asking for financial investment strategies based on industrial intentions and capability data.[28]

This visualization display technology does not rely upon exotic processing technologies. This system simplifies the problem by not trying to fuse all information at once, but instead focuses on fusing the most important data to the on-line trading customer—namely real-time market actions. By focusing one type of data, albeit from five different real-time data sources and formats, it is able to use a simple two-dimensional flat file database that receives real-time data feeds. Proprietary algorithms then translate the raw data into the contextual information on the display.[29] The other data types of company intentions and company capabilities are then readily organized and available "behind" each company's market action topic areas. "Fusion" of the stock market actions, company intentions and company capability data then takes place at the same place where the decisions get made—within the mind of the investor. The broker is no longer the holder of the information making judgments and advising the investor on what actions to take. The investment firm is now a data and information supplier for the investor and is judged by the quality and usefulness of its data for making better decisions.

This surveillance engine is having quite the impact. The website's staffing has grown from an initial cadre of eight to a contingent of 100 to deal with the customer and client volume. Ten major brokerage houses have licenses to provide and use the "Map of the Market" surveillance engine for themselves and their clients, with the latest and most notable new partner being Fidelity Investments.[30]

A New Process?

The process map for the information flow that is occurring relative to this website, if not this entire information industry might look something like this.

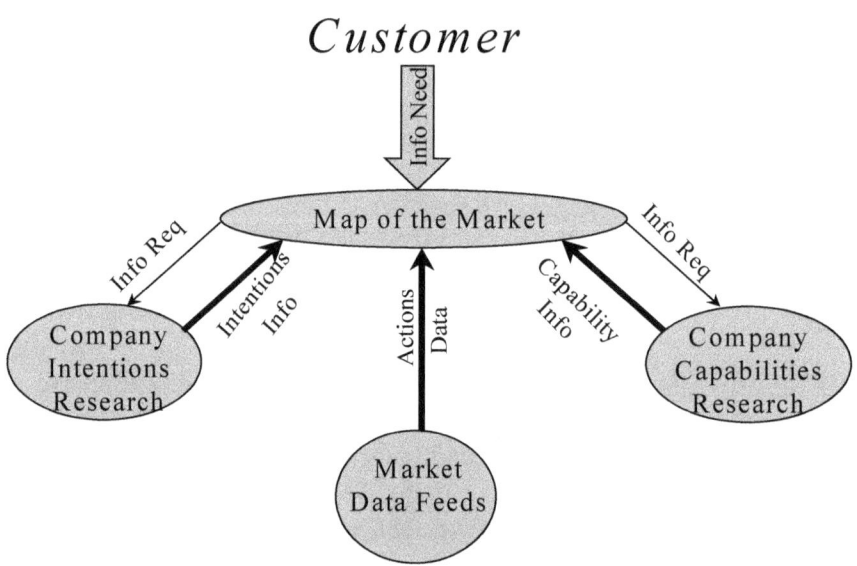

Figure 5 New Information Process?

The website itself is the access point for the customer supplying the market actions data, and based on the customer interaction with the site, tasking is sent requesting certain data to be provided from various research staffs and hyperlinked databases. When the customer clicks on a box to find out more detail about the market actions that are occurring, he is accessing one or more of the real-time "action data" feeds. When he drills down even more to access company strategic plans, or researcher reports on company or competitor manufacturing capacity, he is branching out his information request for supplemental intentions and/or capability information. In essence the display of the market actions data via this surveillance engine off-loads some of the analysis responsibility to the customer. The investor is then able to focus on the area of the market that is important to him. The research staffs are then better able to focus on responding to research questions requiring in-depth analysis and research instead of having to focus on deriving obvious information from the real-time data feeds. In essence the process flow has two branches running at different speeds supplying a single product, information, from three different data categories—market actions, company intentions and company capabilities.

Some might say this "Map of the Market" tool is really no different than Intelink; but, that criticism would miss the point. The smartmoney concept is a way to organize multiple types of data for a fast moving situation. It takes advantage of real time data and captures actions and movements without using pictures, video, or text to get the users attention. It makes the user smarter so he can ask smarter questions of the experts on the other end of the virtual link, and it does it for everyone that has an account—not just a select few of high corporate rank. It is a system that empowers everyone by providing a real-time common operating picture about what is going on right now.

This type of interaction appears to be what today's military customer of ISR data is asking for. He wants real-time access to the raw data and information concerning what is happening, but also wants the ability to tap into a research mechanism to receive personalized instead of institutional service. The current IC process is composed of a single process thread for each intelligence product type and is only able to run at the rate of any one of the serial steps. The roadblocks and time delays used to be processing and the dissemination, but with the IT revolution improvement to both computers and communications, the new problem area is the time it takes a human to do analysis and derive the required actions data from the volumes of intentions and capability data we collect. If a dual rate information process, like the financial industry model, were used as a template for a new IC or space-based ISR information process, and the principles of reengineering and current organizational theory were followed that say structure should be adapted to the new work process flow, then tomorrow's ISR structure might look very different from today's. This analogy has not been lost on our senior military leaders.

> We're not talking simply a "pull" system—one that results in an overwhelming amount of data from which we draw just the tidbits of information we need to start up that continuum to knowledge. Nor are we talking just a "push" system where an analyst tells us what he thinks we need to know. We mean a hybrid—a combination of the best parts of both—enabled through our technology and tailored to fit our requirements. This isn't a new concept, mind you. It's in place and working well in the civilian sector. Take the stock market as an example. Not too long ago we needed a broker to trade stock. We called him up to get information we wanted. If we were lucky, he'd call us back in a couple of days with the results of his research. If we wanted to execute a trade, we called him again. He told us what he thought was promising or perilous, based on where he thought the market was going. And then he carried out our instructions after collecting his commission. Today, we can take one of

these, [a Palm Pilot] and tie into the Internet with access to the portions of the market reports that interest us. With that knowledge, we can execute a transactions directly, at the push of a button. There is no broker telling us what's important, unless we seek him out. We can decide what is important ourselves. . . .We share a "common operational picture," but we tailor it to our individual needs and interests. That's becoming the accepted standard in the civilian market place. . . . I see no reason why we can't do the same for our intelligence systems.[31]

The thing that is missing isn't the appreciation for virtual collaboration or the impact that the IT revolution is having on our culture and our environment. What is missing is a tool to provide the continuous stream of actions data to the military user that would allow a dual rate process to develop, just as it has in the financial industry market. Today's military customer is expecting a 21st Century on-demand fact and information product so they can make decisions and forecasts themselves. Just as warfare and societal structures have had core changes since the 1940s, the process relative to intelligence in also in the process of changing.

While it is unclear what the new information process really looks like at this point, it is does appear that a feature of any new process will be an "on-demand" sort of information system that will allow a customer to do their own research and data gathering, as well as having an "expert opinion" side where questions can be asked and expert answers and projections received. In 1999, a space-based surveillance system was tested in a simulation during the Chief of Staff of the Air Force sponsored Aerospace Futures Capabilities Games in order to test out different variations of a space-based system.[32] If we can simulate the capabilities of a yet to be developed space-based surveillance system, we ought to also be able to simulate a data supply interface for the display of space-based ISR data. The DoD could build this virtual information tasking, dissemination and display system based upon what they think they want. In the past we have relied too much on using what we had instead of trying to strive for what we needed. By taking the initiative to further define the data interface they want, the military customer will be helping to define the interface to himself, instead of having to adapt to the suppliers way of doing business.

With the rise of surveillance, the potential ready access to "actions data," and the customer demands for answers now, the methodical, studious, analytical approach from World War II that is used to derive potential actions from intentions data and capability data is being overwhelmed. The ability to have continuous coverage of the enemy actions will change the process of intelligence analysis.[33] But first we have to get the tool.

Notes

[1] Admiral William A. Owens, USN (Ret.), *Lifting the Fog of War* (New York, N.Y.: Farrar, Straus and Giroux, 2000), 103.

[2] Owens, 104.

[3] Maj Annette L. Totten, USAFR, "The Need for a Revolution in 21st Century Joint Intelligence Collection Management," (masters thesis, Joint Military Intelligence College, August 1999), 62.

[4] IC 21, IV-7-8.

[5] Independent Commission on the National Imagery and Mapping Agency (NIMA Commission), *The Information Edge: Imagery Intelligence and Geospatial Information in an Evolving National Security Environment*, (Washington, D.C.: Government Printing Office, December 2000), 37.

[6] NIMA Commission, 72; and Covault, 67.

[7] Joint Chiefs of Staff, *Joint Publication 2-0, Doctrine for Intelligence Support to Joint Operations*, 9 March 2000, II-1; on-line, Internet, 1 February 2001, available from http://www.dtic.mil/doctrine/jel/new_pubs/jp2_0.pdf.

[8] Central Intelligence Agency, *Factbook on Intelligence* (Washington D.C.: Central Intelligence Agency, 1998), 13.

[9] Richard, 20.

[10] Berkowitz, 69.

[11] Richard, 9.

[12] Richard, 74.

[13] Berkowitz, 22-23.

[14] Richard, 21.

Notes

[15] Stuart Johnson and Martin Libicki, ed., *Dominant Battlespace Knowledge*, (Ft. McNair: National Defense University Press, October 1995); on-line, Internet, 12 December 2000, available from file://S:\DBK%20Book\DBK.htm.

[16] Captain William S. Brei, USAF, *Getting Intelligence Right: The Power of Logical Procedure*, Occasional Paper Number Two (Bolling AFB: Joint Military Intelligence College, January 1996), 4.

[17] Richard, 47.

[18] Berkowitz, 161.

[19] Berkowitz, 164-165.

[20] Myers, 9.

[21] Myers, 16-19.

[22] Berkowitz, 21-22.

[23] Harlan Lebo, *The UCLA Internet Report: Surveying the Digital Future* (Los Angeles Calif.: UCLA Center for Communication Policy, November 2000), 4.

[24] Berkowitz, 22-23.

[25] Adam Cohen, "This Time It's Different," *Time* 157, no. 1 (8 January 2001): 20.

[26] Scitor Corp., "Best Practices Final Report: Information Analysis & Production," June 2000, 18-23.

[27] Lt Col Edward F. Murphy, USAF, et al., "Information Operations: Wisdom Warfare for 2025," in *Air Force 2025, White Papers Volume 1: Awareness*, (Maxwell AFB, Ala.: Air University Press, September 1996), 7.

[28] Jennie Baird, Executive Producer, Smartmoney.com, interviewed by author, 22 February 2001 and 8 March 2001.

[29] Scitor, 21 & 23.

[30] Baird.

[31] Myers, 19-23.

[32] White Paper, AC2ISRC, subject: Space-Based MTI Contributions to Global and Theater Situational Awareness, 26 July 2000, 2.

[33] MAJ Christopher W. Payne, USA, "Tactical Intelligence and Full Spectrum Dominance by 2010: Is it Plausible?" (masters thesis, Joint Military Intelligence College, June 1999), 35.

Chapter 4

Conclusions

If the new definitional construct proposed here for ISR has merit (where different "INTs can be grouped under one of the primary informational components of intentions, capabilities or actions), it becomes clear that while we collect a lot of data through various means, we are greatly lacking in our ability to collect data about an adversary's on-going actions. This type of information is critical for the military customer whose role typically entails having to physically respond in a crisis—not just prepare. In addition, the way we are trying to use information has changed over time due to increases in communication and computer technologies allowing us to get accustom to using "actions data" in our everyday lives. We then bring those experiences to our work environment expecting our current intelligence systems and processes to meet our expectations. Some might advise we adjust our expectations as alluded to in the recent NIMA Commission report.

> The Commission questions whether US military doctrine has evolved to so rely on intelligence—imagery, especially—that it may become unsupportable with current investments. The need to precisely engage— with strategic considerations—any and every tactical target, without collateral damage, without risk to American lives, requires exquisite knowledge immediately prior to, and immediately subsequent to, any strike. Demonstrably, US imagery intelligence cannot support this activity on any meaningful scale without precarious neglect of essential, longer-range issues without additional resources.[1]

47

The choices are to either lower our expectations concerning what the IC can deliver, or make the decisions to try and fix the problems.

As mentioned previously, one option considered for solving the problems relative to space-based ISR has been a merger of NIMA, NRO and NSA. The government has a history of trying to fix problems through structural mergers. An early relevant example is perhaps the circumstances that led to the formation of NSA.

The wartime successes by the US and Britain proved the value of COMINT to political and military leaders.[2] So much so that the military services continued to pursue COMINT separately from one another after World War II despite the evidence that such parochialism had in fact greatly contributed to the surprise attack on Pearl Harbor.[3] "During the Korean War the quality of strategic intelligence derived from COMINT fell below that which had been provided in World War II."[4] This fact, along with service squabbling prompted the creation of the Brownell Committee by President Truman to review the matter. The Brownell Committee recommended that a unified COMINT agency be created, and on 24 October 1952, National Security Council Intelligence Directive No. 9 was revised and signed creating the nation's centralized COMINT agency, NSA, to focus on this critical information category.[5]

The most recent relevant IC structural change was accomplished in October 1996 with the creation of NIMA.[6] Like the creation of NSA in 1952 to consolidate COMINT efforts and fix the problems that resulted from the Korean War, NIMA was formed by merging the similar but disparate imaging analysis efforts that were previously within the Defense Intelligence Agency, the Central Intelligence Agency and the Defense Mapping

Agency in an effort to bring focus to the imagery intelligence processing and dissemination system problems that became evident in the Gulf War.[7]

This history of performing mergers to solve performance problems is probably the impetus for the previous 1996 merger recommendations to solve the current ISR problems; but, the current issues are different from the situations that resulted in the creation of NSA and NIMA. The current ISR problems are not the result of similar activities spread around multiple agencies. The current situation is more akin to the circumstances that resulted in the creation of a coalition between elements of the Air Force and the CIA to solve a technical data collection problem that resulted in the U-2 and the CORONA.[8]

The roots of the current ISR problems are due to an on-going change in the information environment that requires data on what is happening in order to satisfy the customer, and the lack of a space-based tool to supply that data. The Commission to Assess United States National Security Space Management and Organization (AKA: the Space Commission) in its January 2001 would seem to agree with the need to emphasize efforts to build a space-based surveillance system for the collection of "actions data."

> Space provides a unique vantage point for observing objects across vast reaches of air, land and sea. The U.S. needs to develop technologies for sensors, communication, power generations and space platforms that will enable it to observe the earth and objects in motion on a near real-time basis, 24 hours-a-day. If deployed, these could revolutionize military operations. For example, a space-based radar, such as the recently cancelled Discoverer II program, could provide military commanders, on a near-continuous and global basis, with timely, precise information on the location of adversary forces and their movement over time. Coupled to precision strike weapons delivered rapidly over long distances, even conventionally armed inter-continental ballistic missiles, space-based radar surveillance would enhance deterrence of hostile action.[9]

The previous congressional recommendations for a merger between NIMA, NRO and NSA appear to have been rethought. In fact the National Commission for the Review of the National Reconnaissance Office (AKA: the NRO Commission) in its November 2000 report, cautioned against a merger of NIMA, NRO and NSA for fear of losing space-based operations expertise and focus.

> Current divisions of responsibility for the production of imagery intelligence (IMINT), signals intelligence (SIGINT) and measurement and signature (MASINT) intelligence, as well as budget and mission distinctions among the NRO and its mission partners, are not as clear as they should be. To deal with these issues, it was suggested in testimony that NRO SIGINT and IMINT research and development activities, or the entirety of the NRO's SIGINT and IMINT organizations, be assigned to NSA and NIMA, respectively. The Commission believes transfers of SIGINT and IMINT responsibilities from the NRO to NSA and NIMA could be destructive of U.S. capabilities to collect intelligence from space in long run. NSA and NIMA are directly responsible for providing SIGINT and IMINT to U.S. Government officials and military forces. They face voracious current and near-term demands for these products. Thus, budget and program pressures would tempt these agencies to take resources from the development of future space-based capabilities and devote them instead to current collection, analysis and production programs.[10]

The ongoing technology shift for communications technology methods is perhaps another factor that would argue against a merger of these three agencies as explained by Admiral J. M. McConnell, a former Director of NSA.

> Today communications are very different from those of World War II and the Cold War. . . . SIGINT collectors are faced with a networked World that is changing at "internet speed"—i.e., significant changes occur within weeks or months. Over ninety percent of today's communication volume moves through fiber optic cables; a medium that does not radiate radio waves or magnetic signatures into the atmosphere as did those of the past. In addition to being contained inside a fiber optic cable, the complexity of the multiplexing schemes to, literally, "stuff" more and more information into a strand of fiber is staggering; thousands and thousands of communications are active at the same time on one strand of fiber. Imagine 30 to 40 thousand people having telephone conversations on a single strand of fiber with their voices multiplexed in such a way that they are not aware they are sharing the line. In a relatively short period of time,

we have witnessed data volumes for today's communications systems move from a few gigabits—billions—to hundreds of gigabits per seconds. The ability to transmit a terabit—trillions—per second is presently being successfully tested. That would equate to the ability to move the data volume of the library of Congress in minutes.[11]

Primary access to communications data may no longer be the RF energy waves that emanate through our atmosphere and out into space. If this trend holds, the "intentions data" category may in fact need to lessen its expenditure for space-based collection assets. It may instead need to refocus on terrestrial based access to the data, thus bringing into question the role for the NRO relative to building satellites for the collection of "intentions" data and the need for NSA to remain separate from any ISR merger in order to maintain focus on solving its "I" data access problem.

Imaging reconnaissance is also going through changes, but instead of foretelling a reduction in data access, we are potentially going to experience an abundance of pictures due to the number of commercial space-based imaging systems becoming available. A 1999 presentation at DIA estimated that by 2005, 11 new commercial space-based imaging systems would be launched and operated by nine different commercial firms.[12] The Teal Group, a space industry analytical source, estimates that between 2001 and 2010, the total number of new and replacement commercial imaging satellites will reach 43 different systems.[13] Perhaps the most dramatic change is the recent US Government decision to license US firms to provide ½ meter resolution imagery commercially from space instead of limiting the resolution to 1 meter as had been the previous policy.[14] If a large number of high resolution imagery satellite systems do indeed become available during this decade, it could cause us to also question the role of the NRO as the imaging reconnaissance satellite builder for our nation since high resolution imagery will be available from commercial sources.

Even with the potentially dramatic changes to the communication interception and imaging reconnaissance environments, the good news is that today we have established infrastructures led by NSA and NIMA to work the "I" and "R" data categories. What is currently lacking is an infrastructure to work the space-based surveillance issue for space-based ISR with the same vigor as has been done in the past for space-based COMINT and IMINT. Recommendations from the Space Commission in its January 2001 report appear to be taking the first steps to alleviate this void by recommending the merger of all military service and NRO space activities within the Air Force.[15]

> The U.S. Government—in particular, the Department of Defense and the Intelligence Community—is not yet arranged or focused to meet the national security space needs of the 21st century. . . .the Commission concluded that a number of disparate space activities should promptly be merged, chains of command adjusted, lines of communication opened and policies modified to achieve greater responsibility and accountability. Only then can the necessary trade-offs be made, the appropriate priorities be established and the opportunities for improving U.S. military and intelligence capabilities be realized.[16]

This finding and other Space Commission recommendations for the US to pursue a space-based surveillance system were also endorsed by the United States Commission on National Security/21st Century (AKA: the National Security Commission) its January 2001 report.[17]

In the researcher's view, if there is going to be a structural change, this is the structural change to make. By taking such an action, this could help create the infrastructure to focus on developing a space-based system to capture "actions data." While the NRO could still support NSA and NIMA by responding to their requirements for developing and operating space-based "I" and "R" data collection systems, the new joint AF and NRO team could pursue the development and deployment of the needed space-based surveillance system much like the early coalition between the Air Force and CIA produced the U-2 and CORONA.

We should support and implement the findings of the Space Commission and the National Security Commission to develop and deploy a space-based surveillance system and adopt the congressional structural recommendations as a necessary step to align national security space responsibilities and resources to accomplish the task. In the end, what is needed to solve the space-based ISR problems is a data collection and display system to fulfill the age-old desire of the military commander to know what is happening in real-time over the next hill. For the first time in history we are on the verge of being technically capable of fielding such a system from a space-based perch.[18] Until we are able to field such a system, we will not meet the predictions of the military visionaries of attaining a new American way of war. With a recognition of what informational component is missing (namely "actions data"), a viable technical approach to fielding such a system, and national level support to build such a system as evidenced by the recent congressional commissions, we may truly be able to witness the rise of surveillance.

Notes

[1] NIMA Commission, ix.

[2] National Security Agency. *The Origins of NSA*. Fort George G. Meade, Maryland: Center for Cryptologic History, 2000, 2.

[3] Thomas R. Johnson, "The National Security Agency—its Establishment (1952)" (Declassified historical report submitted for publication, September 2000), 1.

[4] *Origins of NSA*, 4.

[5] *Origins of NSA*, 4.

[6] Mohan, 1.

[7] Mohan, 21-22; and Berkowitz, 32-33.

[8] Hall, CORONA, 105, 111-113.

Notes

[9] Commission to Assess United States National Security Space Management and Organization (Space Commission), *The Report of the Commission to Assess United States National Security Space Management and Organization*, 11 January 2001, 31; on-line, Internet, 12 January 2001. Available from http://www.space.gov.

[10] NRO Commission, 29-30.

[11] J. M. McConnell, "The Future of SIGINT: Opportunities and Challenges in the Information Age," *Defense Intelligence Journal: SIGINT* 9, no. 2 (Summer 2000): 45.

[12] McDonald, 76.

[13] Teal Group, "Commercial Imaging Satellites Forecast for 2001-2010," address to the American Institute for Aeronautics and Astronautics/Utah State University Conference on Small Satellites, Logan, Utah, 23 August 2000, 1; on-line, Internet, 11 April 2001, available from http://www.tealgroup.com/pressreleases/imagesats2010.htm

[14] Jason Bates, "U.S. Approves Licenses for Two Imaging Satellites with Half-Meter Resolution," *SPACE.com*, 18 December 2000, n.p.; on-line, Internet, 6 Apr 2001, available from http://www.space.com/businesstechnology/business/satellite_licenses_001218.html

[15] Space Commission, xxiv, 89-92.

[16] Space Commission, ix.

[17] The United States Commission on National Security/21st Century (National Security Commission), *Road Map for National Security: Imperative for Change*, 31 January 2001, 81-82.

[18] AC2ISRC White Paper, 11-12.

Bibliography

Air Force 2025, Air University. USAF Chief of Staff-directed futures study aimed at identifying the concepts, capabilities, and technologies the United States will require to remain the dominant air and space force in the 21st century. Staff study, "Executive Summary," August 1996.

Bates, Jason. "U.S. Approves Licenses for Two Imaging Satellites with Half-Meter Resolution." *SPACE.com*, 18 December 2000, n.p. On-line. Internet, 6 Apr 2001. Available from http://www.space.com/businesstechnology/business/ satellite_licenses_ 001218.html

Berkowitz, Bruce D., and Allan E. Goodman. *Best Truth: Intelligence in the Information Age.* New Haven, Conn.: Yale University Press, 2000.

Brei, Captain William S., USAF, *Getting Intelligence Right: The Power of Logical Procedure.* Occasional Paper Number Two. Bolling AFB: Joint Military Intelligence College, January 1996.

Burrows, William E. *Deep Black.* New York, N.Y.: Random House Inc., 1986.

Camden, Alan D. "Communications Support to Intelligence." In *The First Information War.* Edited by Alan D. Camden. Fairfax, V.A.: AFCEA International Press, October 1992.

Carter, CAPT Clarence E., USN, et al. "The Man in the Chair: Cornerstone of Global Battlespace Dominance." In *Air Force 2025, White Papers Volume 1: Awareness.* Maxwell AFB, Ala.: Air University Press, September 1996.

Central Intelligence Agency. *Factbook on Intelligence.* Washington D.C.: Central Intelligence Agency, 1998.

Cohen, Adam. "This Time It's Different." *Time* 157, no. 1 (8 January 2001): 18-22.

Commission on the Roles and Capabilities of the United States Intelligence Community. *Preparing for the 21st Century: An Appraisal of U.S. Intelligence.* Washington, D.C.: Government Printing Office, 1 March 1996. On-line. Internet, 31 August 2000. Available from http://www.access.gpo.gov/intelligence/int/index.html.

Commission to Assess United States National Security Space Management and Organization. *The Report of the Commission to Assess United States National Security Space Management and Organization*, 11 Jan 2001. On-line. Internet, 12 January 2001. Available from http://www.space.gov.

Cooper, Jeffrey R. "Strategy." In *Air and Space Power in the New Millennium.* Edited by Daniel Goure' and Christopher M. Szara. Washington D.C.: Center for Strategic and International Studies, 1997.

Corcoran, Maj Kimberly M., USAF. "Higher Eyes in the Sky: The Feasibility of Moving AWACS and JSTARS Functions into Space." Masters thesis, School of Advanced Air Power Studies, October 1999.

Covault, Craig. "NIMA Infotech Retools U.S. Space Recon Ops." *Aviation Week and Space Technology*, 7 August 2000, 63-67.

Defense News, 23 October 2000.

Foglesong, Capt David H., USAF, "Intelligence, Dominant Battlespace Knowledge, and the Warfighter." Masters thesis, Joint Military Intelligence College, August 1998.

Hall, R. Cargill. "Postwar Strategic Reconnaissance and the Genesis of CORONA." In *Eye in the Sky: The Story of the CORONA Spy Satellites*. Edited by Dwayne A. Day, John M. Logsdon and Brian Latell. Washington D.C.: Smithsonian Institution Press, August 1999.

Hall, R. Cargill. "From Concept to National Policy: Strategic Reconnaissance in the Cold War." *Prologue: Quarterly of the National Archives and Records Administration* 28, no. 2 (Summer 1996): 107-125.

Hall, R. Cargill. "The Eisenhower Administration and the Cold War: Framing American Astronautics to Serve National Security." *Prologue: Quarterly of the National Archives and Records Administration* 27, no. 1 (Spring 1995): 59-72.

Hammer, Michael, and James Champy. *Reengineering the Corporation: A Manifesto for Business* Revolution. New York, N.Y.: Harper Collins Publishers, Inc.,1994.

Harlow, Ensign Keith E., USN. "Information Overload in Surface Combatants: A Role for Data Warehousing?" Masters thesis, Joint Military Intelligence College, August 1998.

Hayden, Lt Gen Michael V., USAF, Director National Security Agency. Address. Kennedy Political Union of American University, Washington D.C., 17 February 2000.

Hayden, Michael V. "The Change Imperative." *Defense Intelligence Journal: SIGINT* 9, no. 2 (Summer 2000): 27-37.

House Permanent Select Committee on Intelligence, *IC 21: Intelligence Community in the 21st Century*, 104th Cong. Washington, D.C.: Government Printing Office, 9 April 1996, 2-6 of 25. On-line. Internet, 31 August 2000. Available from http://www.access.gpo.gov/congress/house/intel/ic21/ic21_cov.html.

Independent Commission on the National Imagery and Mapping Agency. *The Information Edge: Imagery Intelligence and Geospatial Information in an Evolving National Security Environment*, Final Report, December 2000. On-line. Internet, 12 January 2001. Available from http://www.space.gov.

Johnson, Stuart and Martin Libicki, ed. *Dominant Battlespace Knowledge*. Ft. McNair: National Defense University Press, October 1995. On-line. Internet, 12 December 2000. Available from file://S:\DBK%20Book\DBK.htm.

Johnson, Thomas R. "The National Security Agency—its Establishment (1952)." Declassified historical report submitted for publication, September 2000.

Joint Staff, Director for Strategic Plans and Policy, J-5. *Joint Vision 2020*. Washington D.C.: Government Printing Office, June 2000.

Joint Chiefs of Staff. *Joint Publication 2-0, Doctrine for Intelligence Support to Joint Operations*, 9 March 2000, II-1. On-line. Internet, 1 February 2001. Available from http://www.dtic.mil/doctrine/jel/new_pubs/jp2_0.pdf.

Lebo, Harlan. *The UCLA Internet Report: Surveying the Digital Future*. Los Angeles Calif.: UCLA Center for Communication Policy, November 2000.

Marshall, Maj James P., USAF, "Near Real-Time Intelligence of the Tactical Battlefield." In *Theater Air Campaign Studies*, Edited by Maj Pat Battles. Maxwell AFB, Ala.: Air University Press, 1995.

McConnell, J. M. "The Future of SIGINT: Opportunities and Challenges in the Information Age." *Defense Intelligence Journal: SIGINT* 9, no. 2 (Summer 2000): 39-49.

McDonald, Robert A. "NRO's Satellite Imaging Reconnaissance: Moving from the Cold War Threat to Post-Cold War Challenges." *Defense Intelligence Journal: IMINT* 8, no. 1 (Summer 1999): 55-91.

McLucas, John L. Address. Air Force Historical Foundation Symposium, Andrews AFB, MD, 21-22 September 1995. "The U.S. Space Program Since 1961." In *The U.S. Air Force in Space, 1945 to the 21st Century*. Edited by R. Cargill Hall and Jacob Neufeld. Washington, D.C.: Government Printing Office, 1998.

Mohan, Jim. "Tracing NIMA's Roots." 15 September 2000.

Murphy, Lt Col Edward F., USAF, et al. "Information Operations: Wisdom Warfare for 2025." In *Air Force 2025, White Papers Volume 1: Awareness*. Maxwell AFB, Ala.: Air University Press, September 1996.

Myers, Gen Richard B. Myers, USAF, vice chairman joint chiefs of staff. Address. Defense Intelligence Agency, Washington D.C., 18 September 2000.

National Commission for the Review of the National Reconnaissance Office. *The NRO at the Crossroads*, 1 November 2000. On-line. Internet, 29 November 2000. Available from http://www.nrocommission.com.

National Security Agency. *The Origins of NSA*. Fort George G. Meade, Maryland: Center for Cryptologic History, 2000.

Norman, Lt Col James O., Air Force Fellow, memorandum to NIMA/CITO, subject: Tasking Statistics for Use in Research Paper (U), 1 March 2001. (Secret/TK) Information extracted is unclassified.

New York Times, 12 May 1999.

Owens, Admiral William A., USN (Ret.). *Lifting the Fog of War*. New York, N.Y.: Farrar, Straus and Giroux, 2000.

Payne, MAJ Christopher W., USA, "Tactical Intelligence and Full Spectrum Dominance by 2010: Is it Plausible?" Masters thesis, Joint Military Intelligence College, June 1999).

Peebles, Curtis. *High Frontier: The U.S. Air Force and the Military Space Program*. Washington, D.C.: Government Printing Office, 1997.

Perry, Robert L. *Management of the National Reconnaissance Program 1960-1965*. Washington D.C.: NRO History Office, 1969.

RAND, *Project Air Force: 1999 Annual Report*.

Richard, Maj Dana G., USAFR, "United States Joint Intelligence in World War II—Its Organization and Effectiveness as Determined by Its Contribution to Allied Information Superiority." Masters thesis, Joint Military Intelligence College, August 1999.

Ruffner, Kevin C., ed. *CORONA: America's First Satellite Program*. Washington D.C.: History Staff, Center for the Study of Intelligence, Central Intelligence Agency, 1995.

Scitor Corp. "Best Practices Final Report: Information Analysis & Production." June 2000.

Shulsky, Abram N. and Gary J. Schmitt. *Silent Warfare: Understanding the World of Intelligence*, 2nd ed. New York N.Y.: Macmillan Publishing Company, 1993.

Singh, Simon. *The Code Book*. New York, N.Y.: Random House Inc., 1999.

Space News, 16 October 2000.

Swalm, Thomas L. "Joint STARS in Desert Storm." In *The First Information War*. Edited by Alan D. Camden. Fairfax, V.A.: AFCEA International Press, October 1992.

Teal Group. "Commercial Imaging Satellites Forecast for 2001-2010." Address. American Institute for Aeronautics and Astronautics/Utah State University Conference on Small Satellites, Logan, Utah, 23 August 2000, 1. On-line. Internet, 11 April 2001. Available from http://www.tealgroup.com/pressreleases/imagesats 2010.htm

Totten, Maj Annette L., USAFR, "The Need for a Revolution in 21st Century Joint Intelligence Collection Management." Masters thesis, Joint Military Intelligence College, August 1999.

The United States Commission on National Security/21st Century, *Road Map for National Security: Imperative for Change*, 31 January 2001.

Washington Post, 17 October 2000.

Washington Post, 17 November 2000.

Washington Post, 20 November 2000.

White Paper. AC2ISRC. Subject: Space-Based MTI Contributions to Global and Theater Situational Awareness, 26 July 2000.